GET THAT JOB!

Ace Your Job Interview – Every Time!

Christine Reidhead

Christine Reidhead is an Assistant Professor of Business and Chair of the Business and Education Department at Navajo Technical University.

She is a Doctoral Candidate at Grand Canyon University in Leadership and Organizational Development. She has her Master's in Accountancy from the University of Phoenix.

Christine has been working at a Tribal College for over seven years and is the Founder and CEO of AfrikRising Nonprofit Organization and Podcaster.

Table Of Contents

INTRODUCTION

Landing a job in this contemporary job market is becoming more difficult than ever, as there are more people going out of their way to learn new skills and become better qualified for the same job position you are seeking. The competition is stiff.

As a result, having a well-crafted resume is just the first step toward landing your dream job, because your potential employer is aware that many people seek out professional help to write their resume. You also have to convince your potential employer that out of the numerous candidates whose resumes have been selected, you are the best candidate for the job. That is what an interview is all about. And trust me, there is a lot more to it than just meeting with the person in charge of hiring, and introducing yourself to your potential employer.

A job interview is an opportunity for you to sell yourself to your interviewer, and you need to prepare well so you can give it your very best shot. It is one thing to be qualified for the job, but it is quite another thing to convince someone else with very clear descriptions that you are not only qualified but also the *most* qualified of all the candidates invited to interview for the same position.

An interview can be a very intimidating process for the interviewee, which justifies the fact that many job seekers are always very nervous and have little confidence in themselves no matter how qualified they are for the position. If you feel intimidated, you are not alone; it is absolutely normal. You are meeting experts in the field you have applied to, and it is understandable if you feel less confident. But you have to do something to acquire the confidence you need to excel in your interview, because you cannot afford to miss this opportunity to sell yourself and land that job.

Does all this sound scary?

Don't worry. In the following chapters of this book, I will take you through a step-by-step guide on how to prepare for a job interview. By the time you get to the last chapter, you will have learned what to do before the interview, during the interview, and even after the interview. With this book, you can be assured of building enough confidence to do well in any kind of interview and land yourself a good job.

Let's get started.

CHAPTER ONE

Types of Job Interviews

There are different types of interviews according to what works best for the recruiter. The different types are usually dependent on the location of the interview, the time factor, and what the recruiter intends to achieve with the interview. As the candidate, you should prepare beforehand for all types of interviews so you are ready for whatever the recruiter chooses. The three main types of interviews are as follows:

- Face-to-face interview

- Telephone interview

- Video interview

Let's explore them in detail.

Face-to-Face Interview

This is the traditional and most common type of interview, where you are invited to the company or another venue chosen by the company to have a one-on-one interaction with them. It is usually the most intimidating of all interviews because most likely you are meeting these people for the first time and you are not sure what kind of questions they will ask. Therefore, you need to be prepared and exude confidence.

The following steps can help you overcome your fears and go into the interview room with confidence and ready for anything.

- **Research the company:** The first thing you need to do is your research. You should know not only the company but also the industry and, if possible, your interviewer(s). When you are answering the questions you are asked, you need to find a way to talk about the company and make examples with the company so the recruiter knows you are truly interested in them and have done your homework. Google them, or ask current or former employees about the company. But please ensure that you do proper research before showing up to the interview.

- **Research the role:** The next thing you should research is the job description. No matter how knowledgeable or experienced you may be in the particular job area, you still have to do proper research on that position in relation to the particular company that is interviewing you. Make a connection between yourself, the position, the company, and the industry at large.

- **Look the part:** As the old saying goes, dress the way you want to be addressed. This is especially true when you are going before a person or some persons who are outright assessing everything about you to decide if you are a fit for the position. Look your best. Put on some professional clothing that will give off an air of seriousness. If you are female, do not wear very high heels that announce your arrival even before the receptionist looks up to see you. Everything should be in moderation, including your makeup. If you are a guy, make sure you are clean-shaven. And, generally, do not wear strong perfume or cologne that may be offensive to the recruiter.

- **Control bad habits:** If you are a smoker, alcohol addict, or someone who is always chewing, you will have to make do without these for the period of your face-to-face interview. Alcohol and smoke have stenches that people around you will perceive more than you do, and you never can tell how bad you smell until some honest person around you opens up to you. You don't want to enter the interview room smelling of alcohol.

- **Prepare for a test:** A face-to-face interview may come with a test, and your score will be recorded as part of your interview performance. Your research about the role, the company, and the industry will help you out in such a case. But you should also brush up on your logic and critical thinking skills in case there is an aptitude test.

There is a lot more about best practices for the face-to-face interview in the following chapters, since it is the most common of the three types of job interviews.

Telephone Interview

Some recruiters may choose to interview you over the phone, to save time, cost, or both. Whatever the case, you should be prepared and perform well to land the job. A telephone interview is usually scheduled, but sometimes the interviewer may decide to catch you off guard to find out how well you can perform in an impromptu situation.

Also, a telephone interview may be the main interview before you are told whether you are getting the job or not, but some companies also conduct the telephone interview only as a screening process in order to select the best candidates for the final interview. Whatever, the case, don't discount the phone interview or any communication with the company before you get the job. You want to make a good impression with every point of contact.

If the recruiter decides to have a telephone interview with you, it could be to your advantage because you will have less information to worry about. You will save time and the effort you would have spent traveling to the interview venue, and you won't have to worry about your physical appearance. That's great, but do not get too relaxed. Remember, it is still an interview, and your performance most likely is going to determine whether the company wants to continue the interview process.

For a telephone interview, this is how to prepare to be the best candidate for the job:

- **Know what to expect:** Know that one of the basic qualities that will be assessed is your telephone etiquette. Are you well mannered? Are you polite? Do you sound smart? Will you be able to be a good ambassador of the company if you are representing them over the phone? These are verbal qualities you should prepare and be ready to present when you are called.

- **Be ready and relaxed:** Ensure that you are mentally prepared, especially if the interview was scheduled. You should have no excuse. If the interview was not scheduled and you are very busy when the call comes, excuse yourself for a few minutes and pull yourself together. Try not to be too nervous; it's only a job interview.

- **Make the conversation engaging:** Do not answer in monosyllables. Allow your interviewer to keep the conversation going. When you are asked a question, give a clear explanation and vivid descriptions. That way, your interviewer will be convinced that you actually know what you are talking about. If there is anything about yourself that you would like the interviewer to know, look for an interesting way to bring it into the conversation. And when you are explaining or describing, give real instances to back up your points.

- **Don't be distracted:** Stay focused and remain interested in the conversation. If you are distracted, your interviewer can tell. Do not give them the impression that the position is not important to you. This is not the time for you to show your multitasking skills; just drop everything else and remain attentive to the conversation while making intelligent contributions.

Video Interview

Video interviews are becoming more and more popular because they save time and cost and collapse the barriers of time and location. This, like the telephone interview, does not involve a physical meeting. But unlike the telephone interview, the interviewer will see you talk. In the video interview, you have a lot of preparations to make as if you are preparing for a face-to-face interview.

No professional will call you for a video interview without scheduling it first, so you will always have enough time to prepare and build your confidence. Let's talk about how best to prepare for a video interview and land that job:

- **Get the necessary equipment ready:** The first thing to do in preparation for a video interview is to get the required technology ready. It is highly advisable that you do not use the built-in camera on your laptop. The built-in camera is usually poor quality. Get an external camera and a microphone. It is important that your interviewer sees you and hears you clearly enough that they do not have to strain their eyes or ears. Make sure you have a good internet connection; you definitely do not want an on-and-off connection during your interview session.

This is not a good time to use your Wi-Fi. Please use a better option, as this can be a choppy service and unreliable. And when you have completed setting up the necessary equipment, test it to ensure it is actually working.

- **Get a professional username:** Your username for whatever video platform you are using should be professional. You do not want a username such as: @wildsam24. This will be inappropriate to use and unprofessional. You could use your first and last name, or first name initial and last name. You don't want to leave the recruiter with the impression that you are not a serious person. Some recruiters may not care about your username, but some others will consider it part of your assessment. To be on the safe side, whether you are a serious person or not, for the sake of this interview, pretend to be a serious candidate.

- **Make arrangements for a comfortable venue:** Another very important part of your video interview is the venue. You may not be meeting the recruiter at a physical venue, but they will get to see not only you but also your background. You need to make sure everything is in place behind you before your interview kicks off. Pick a good spot and make sure there is nothing unprofessional in the background. If you have roommates or you are living with your family, you have to give everyone a heads-up that you have a video interview coming up and let them know you need quiet during that time. Let them know you are serious about it, or even get them involved in your preparation process so they will understand how important it is to you.

- **Go for a better alternative:** If you can't ensure you will have privacy at home during the interview period, you can book a room at a cheap hotel in your neighborhood strictly for the interview. If the job is important to you, then it is definitely worth the effort and expense. Make sure the room is well lit.

- **Dress the part:** Granted, this is not a face-to-face interview, but technically, it actually is. Do not assume that the interviewer will only get a view of your face, and dress like you would for a real in-person interview. If the position you are interviewing for requires a formal outfit, wear a formal outfit. Even if the position does not require a formal outfit, still do not dress too casually. Show the interviewer you have put in the effort.

- **Have good posture:** Your posture is very important. As the interview is going on, you want to maintain eye contact with the interviewer. To do so, do not look into the eyes of the interviewer on the screen. Instead, look into the camera. If there are questions you have prepared beforehand, write them down on sticky notes and place them just beside the camera. You don't want to be looking down to get questions while the interview is going on.

- **Get a good chair:** Do not use a swivel chair. A stationary chair is recommended. If you are using a swivel chair, you may start turning from one side to the next, and the interviewer will see your nervousness.

CHAPTER TWO

3 Stages of the Interview Process and How Best to Behave at Each Stage

You now know the types of interviews to expect and the best practices for each type. Next are the stages of the interview process and how best to present yourself at each stage. These stages are primarily for face-to-face interviews, but most of the practices here also apply to the other types of interviews. The interview does not begin the moment you are in front of your interviewer, nor does it end immediately when you leave the interview venue. To give your job interview your best shot, you must prepare and take every stage seriously, so at the end of the day you are satisfied with the fact that you have done your best. Do not only tell the recruiter that you are the best, but also be the best.

Here are the stages of the job interview process and how to present yourself at each stage.

Before the Interview

- Before the scheduled date of the interview, you need to get yourself ready both physically and psychologically and ensure that nothing will steal your confidence. Try not to engage in quarrels or arguments. In fact, you should be so busy preparing for your interview that you do not have time for any negative behavior.

- Do not wait until the night before the interview to get together the things you need. Always prepare early because something may come up at any moment and complicate your plans. Get your stuff ready and have a good night's rest the night before the interview. You shouldn't appear before the recruiter looking tired or exhausted.

- Make sure you have a copy of your resume and other materials you think you may need or have been asked to bring. Print them out and put them neatly in a file. You want to impress the interviewer.

- Look the part. This point should not be belabored, because I believe you already know you should look good when you present yourself—a job interview should not be an exception. But you are not only trying to look good, you are also trying to look the part. This may sound like a theatrical performance, and the truth is, it actually is a performance, just not in the theater. You should perform before your interviewer in such a natural way that they will not realize you are performing. Put on the best outfit for the occasion. Find out the theme color of the company and the type of attire the staff wear. Then you can choose your interview clothing according to your findings.

- Go early for your interview. You should not be late for your interview; that gives the worst first impression you could ever give your interviewer. If you are a heavy sleeper, make sure you set your alarm and keep it very close to your bed so you can wake up on time and arrive early for your interview. But though it is best practice to arrive early for your interview, you should avoid getting there too early. Don't walk into the interview venue thirty minutes before the time scheduled. You will only appear desperate and also give the company the impression that you are idle and not making the best use of your time. It is advisable that you arrive in the vicinity of the interview venue by thirty minutes before the appointment but only walk into the venue about ten or fifteen minutes before the scheduled time. Though you really want the job, you don't want to appear desperate.

- When you arrive at the venue of the interview, which you should have located earlier and have no difficulty finding, put on your best attitude. Put on a smile and make sure to say hello to the reception staff. It goes without saying that you should not be rude to the receptionist. Even if for some reason the receptionist is having a bad day and you are not received well, ignore the manner of whoever is attending to you and focus your mind on the reason you are there. Everything else is an unnecessary distraction.

- Switch off your phone before you enter the interview venue. Do not put it on vibrate or silent mode; switch it off. Besides the fact that your phone should not ring during the interview, you should not be seen chatting on social media or smiling into your phone as you are waiting in the reception area. You may not be able to control it because if you are an average twenty-first-century youth, you probably have some kind of addiction to social media and will always log in to Facebook or Instagram subconsciously. The best option is to switch it off.

- If you are asked to wait, wait patiently without complaining or looking bored and frustrated. In a case where you are kept waiting for a while, you will definitely get bored, especially when your phone is switched off. But never succumb to the temptation of coming to the interview venue with your earpiece or headphones to listen to music while you wait. Instead, you can take a book and glance at the pages while you wait. You may want to read from your phone, but nobody will know what you are actually doing with the phone, and they can assume anything at your expense. To be on the safe side, put your phone away. Go with a book instead.

During the Interview

So you are finally called in for your interview and you are eager to give it your best shot. Here are tips on how best to achieve excellence during your job interview session:

- You have prepared for this moment, and it is time to prove yourself. Walk into the interview room confidently. Your posture and body language manner are important. You should never slouch. Remember, you have less than ten seconds to make a first impression, and the time does not start when you are seated and being interviewed; it begins right from the moment you enter the room. Give the impression that you are the kind of person the interviewer wouldn't mind spending time with.

- Extend a hand and have a firm handshake with your interviewer. Do it with confidence and not as if you are afraid. It is just an interview, and you either get the job or you do not. Having this mindset will help you have the kind of confidence you need to face your interviewer and perform well in your interview. It is also important to note that if your face-to-face interview is with a panel and not a single interviewer, you can say hello to the group and forget about handshakes, unless one of them extends their hand first. It may be awkward going around—depending on their seating arrangement—to have a handshake with the whole panel of interviewers, so just say hello with a bold smile and take your seat.

- Maintain eye contact throughout the interview. This is not the time to admire the artwork on the walls or analyze the design of the ceiling. You should focus on the business of the day and make sure your interviewer sees that eagerness in you. If you are the shy type and have difficulty maintaining eye contact with people, you should ensure you have a mock interview beforehand and practice maintaining eye contact.

- If you are given a swivel chair, you may be tempted to or even absentmindedly swing from side to side. This is another reason you should have a mock interview before your actual interview. Practice sitting on a swivel chair and talking with someone without swinging from side to side.

- Every good company wants happy staff, which also implies that they are going to hire happy people. Your cheerfulness and smile should not expire after you have made your first impression. You should maintain it. It is true that a job interview is serious business and requires seriousness, but even in your seriousness, smile and be cheerful. The interviewer will not remember the interview as serious business while scoring you low in this aspect. Do not appear sad or negative. Look cheerful always.

- In as much as you should exude cheerfulness during your interview session, you should also try not to appear too excited. Even if you have done your research and, from your findings, the company is what you want from a workplace, you have to be careful not to get so carried away that you get distracted from the main goal of the day. Be cheerful, but don't be too excited; overexcitement could be interpreted as desperation. And, trust me, most companies do not want to hire a desperate interviewee.

- When you are asked questions, do not give answers in monosyllables. It should be an interaction, and part of what you are being interviewed for is your ability to carry on a reasonable conversation. Give it your best. Give detailed descriptions. You should have rehearsed how to answer some questions about yourself, the company, and the position you are being interviewed for, and you should have some relevant stories you can use to make your illustrations as vivid as possible.

- In a case where you are underqualified for the position or do not have the required level of experience, you have the opportunity to show your potential in place of your experience, and you really need to prepare for this. Practice, rehearse, and do a mock interview with a friend or family member to see how well you will perform.

- Avoid giving an off-the-subject answer to any question you are asked. If you do not understand the question, ask your interviewer to rephrase it. It is better for you to be sincere than to give the impression that you understand the question only to end up giving an answer that does not even come close. By doing so, you give your interviewer the impression that you are not bold enough or sincere enough to ask for clarifications when you are unsure. That is not a good quality. Don't worry, the interviewer understands that you are not perfect. Even the best candidates give a less-than-stellar performance sometimes. Answer the questions you understand and seek clarifications for the ones you do not understand. If you give an unclear answer to a question because you do not understand it, you will lose some points; but if you open up, get some clarification, and give an intelligent answer, the recruiter may not even remember that you didn't get the question at first.

- When you are asked if you have any questions, your answer should be yes, and you should ask reasonable questions. It is expected that you will have some questions prepared beforehand from your research about the company. Asking intelligent questions will endear you to your interviewers and increase your chances of being selected for the position. Questions such as: What qualities would an ideal applicant for this position possess? What does a typical day look like for someone in this position? How would you describe the company culture? How do you measure success for this position? What are your expectations for the person in this role for the first month, six months, and year? Avoid discussing salary early in the interview. Do not ask about remuneration until you have clarified other areas. You need find out how much the position is worth, but you should also be careful so you do not appear as if you are interested only in the money and not about the value you will bring to the team.

After the Interview

When you are done with the interview, you have completed most of what you need to do. But the game is not over yet. There is still something else to do. What you do after the interview is as important as what you do before and during the interview, because the recruiter's final decision may even be based on your overall attitude, including your attitude after the interview. And if you do not get it right, all the preparations you have done will be wasted. Here are some important things you should do after your interview:

- As soon as the interview ends, ask your interviewer how you should follow up, and get the contact details of the person or persons that interviewed you. You will need that information for sending thank-you notes.

- Send your interviewer a thank-you note or email. If it was a phone or video interview, there was no physical contact, so a thank-you email would suffice. But in a case of a face-to- face interview, mailing a physical thank-you note is also a good idea. You will be giving your recruiter something to remember you by. In the note, express your gratitude for being given the opportunity for an interview and thank your interviewer for taking the time to interview you.

- Usually, you will learn a thing or two from your new interview experience, and you should write these things down for future reference. Also write down anything that skipped your mind or any question you wish you had asked during the interview. If you do this, these things will easily come to mind in case of another interview.

- Ask the recruiters the timeline for feedback so you will know when to get back to them should they forget to get back to you. On a general note, it is advisable that you follow up a week after the interview if you do not hear from the company. And please be polite. It can be frustrating when you are interviewed and you do not get as much feedback from the recruiters as you would have liked, irrespective of whether it is positive or negative feedback. But your frustration should not reflect in the follow-up email you send. Simply remind them of the interview and ask for feedback as politely as possible.

- It is common for people to share their everyday life experiences on social media. If you do this, your interview experience should not be among the life experiences you share, especially if the experience isn't a good one. Your recruiter could be following social media, and you are at risk of warding off potential recruiters if you share your interview experience. Recruiters are fully aware that young people spend a good number of hours on social media every day, so they are watching. Build a good social media profile for yourself and present yourself the way you would love to be perceived.

- Now that we are talking about social media, it is also a smart step for you to follow up with your interviewers on LinkedIn. Most serious professionals have a LinkedIn profile, so you can find them through the contact details you collect from them. Present yourself on LinkedIn exactly the way you present yourself during a job interview. There are so many resources on the internet that can help you tweak your LinkedIn profile, which will give you a better chance of being taken seriously.

- If you receive negative feedback, it shouldn't change your attitude toward the company. Still write them another thank-you email thanking them for having considered you for an interview. You are doing that to present the message that you are a good person and your character is stable and not affected by temporary circumstances.

Chapter Three

12 Most Common Job Interview Questions and How Best to Answer Them

No two job interviews are the same. But job interviews generally follow a similar pattern with similar questions. You need to arm yourself with the kind of questions you should expect and the best response for each question. Recruiters are also aware of the fact that there are many blogs out there with the title "How to Answer Job Interview Questions," and they can tell when you are merely reciting what you have memorized from another source. In other words, this is a guide on how to answer the questions and not exactly how you should answer the questions. I am giving you a pattern and some strategies. You should tailor them to fit your own personal experiences. Here are some of the most common job interview questions and how to answer them:

- **Tell Us About Yourself:**

This is usually the first question, and it is asked by practically all job interviewers. You should expect it and prepare for it beforehand. It is, however, not an invitation for you to summarize your resume; they have seen your resume already and still want to know more about you. You should talk about your background; and by background, I do not mean your family background and personal life history. Don't mention your marital status or any other personal matters, including religious or political views. No matter how beautiful your family story may be, do not share it, because that is not what they want to hear. Summarize your educational history in no more than three sentences, and talk about your professional experience if you have any. This is the time to clarify the gaps on your resume if you have any. Talk about your skills as they relate to the position, and say a thing or two about your personality. All these should be in line with the role you are being interviewed for. And you should stop talking if you are cut short while you are still answering.

- **What Do You Consider to Be Your Biggest Professional Achievement?**

  This question can be a tough one, especially if you just graduated from college and haven't had any professional experience. Preparing for this question will allow you to give a good response. This is an opportunity for you to talk about your internship experience if you have any and what you consider to be your biggest achievement in the process. Do not just give a vague mention of the achievement; give a vivid description of what you actually did and how it helped the company or team you worked with. Talk about results; that's what the recruiter wants to hear.

- What Are Your Biggest Weaknesses?

  For every question you will answer, remember that you should provide answers in line with what you are interviewing for. If you are asked what your biggest weaknesses are, make sure you state your professional weaknesses, not your general weaknesses as a person. Another thing to note is that at each stage of the interview, you are marketing yourself, and you shouldn't say anything that will vilify you. You should not tell lies. However, if your biggest professional weaknesses are not something you wish to disclose, you should consider saying something else, whether it is the biggest of your weaknesses or not. Pick a weakness of yours and embellish it in such a way that it will eventually turn out interesting. Consider this example from www.inc.com:

Interviewer: What are your biggest weaknesses?

Interviewee: My biggest weakness is getting so absorbed in my work that I lose track of time. Every day I look up and realize everyone has gone home! I know I should be more aware of the clock, but when I love what I am doing, I just can't think of anything else.

In other words, your biggest weakness is that you will put in more hours at work and that will be considered a strength for the company.

You can also talk about a weakness you are currently working on and give brief details about the steps you have taken to improve in that area. That way, the interviewer will consider you as someone who goes out of their way to look for solutions to problems.

- **What Are Your Biggest Strengths?**

  This is practically the opposite of the previous question, "What are your biggest weaknesses?" and you have to be careful with answers here as well. You should state what your biggest strengths are, but do it in such a way that you will not present yourself as a super human. Simply say what your actual professional strengths are and demonstrate with a short description how that strength has helped solve a work-related problem in the past. For instance, if your biggest strength is effective communication, give an instance of when you used that skill to get something done or get other people to do things. And remember to give a sincere answer.

- **What Motivates You?**

There is no right or wrong answer to this question. But, then, this is a job interview, and you need to impress your interviewer. So like every other question you will answer on this interview, tailor your answer to the role you are interviewing for. You should mention positive things that motivate you, like having to meet deadlines, being a part of a team, being a leader, discovering and learning new things, etc.

- **Where Do You See Yourself in the Next Five Years?**

  This question can be challenging, especially if you do not have long-term career plans. But always remember that you are answering in relation to the position you are interviewing for and avoid mentioning anything outside this. This is not the time to talk about the vacation you have been imagining or how much money you expect to have in your bank account by that time. Talk about how you intend to grow from the experience you will receive from the role and some value you expect to add to the company. Give realistic goals and how the position will enhance your chances of reaching them.

- **What Do You Know About This Company?**

  This is a straightforward question, which means the interviewer expects you to have done your homework about the company. Describe what you have found out about the company in relation to its competitors and the industry at large. But do not mention if their competitors are doing better than them. Highlight how the company is doing, especially in the area of the position you are interviewing for and how you think it is the best place for you to pursue a career.

- **How Did You Find Out About This Opening?**

  This kind of question is another opportunity for you to show you are interested in the company and not just in getting a job. Your response should be specifically about how you found out about the opening. Even if you learned about it through a random job search, try to tell the interviewer(s) what caught your attention about this particular opening and how excited you were when you received an invitation to interview.

- **What Type of Work Environment Do You Prefer?**

  This shouldn't be a difficult question to answer if you have done your homework about the company.

Simply bring in the work culture of the company and how it connects to the position you are interviewing for. It shouldn't be about you alone, but about how the kind of work environment you prefer will help you be more successful in your role and add value to the company.

- **Why Do You Want This Job?**

  Well, why do you want the job? A very simple question, but the way you respond will go a long way toward determining the outcome of your interview. Just like every other question you will answer, this should be about the role as well and your overall career growth and development. You should never say you want the job because you are broke and need the salary—whether this is the true situation or not. Explain how the role and how it is represented in the company fits into your personal career plans. Explain how you think the company has the kind of environment that will enhance your growth and push you forward in your career.

- **What Is Your Salary Expectation?**

  This question can make you very uncomfortable, and you may find yourself in between trying not to oversell yourself and also trying not to undersell yourself. If you mention a large salary, you could come across to the interviewer as arrogant. If you ask for a small salary instead, you could come across as undervalued, and the quality of what you have to offer will be in doubt. The best way to go about this is to know beforehand the average salary of the position you are interviewing for. Do your research and find out what the position is worth. Then go ahead and give a salary range. Do not mention a specific amount; that is too direct. Also let your interviewer know you are flexible on the salary expectation and it is left for you to accept or reject what they offer you. Another way to answer the salary expectation question is to tell the interviewer that you are okay with the company's budget for the position. But if you say this, also make sure you are willing to accept what they have to offer.

- **Why Should We Hire You?**

This question sums up everything about the interview. "Now that you have told us all of this, what other reason do you think that, out of all the candidates being interviewed for this position, we should hire you?" This is an opportunity for you to sell yourself. Emphasize not only how you can do the job, but also how you can do it better than any other candidate. Talk about your most important skills and how you can produce results within the company culture.

CHAPTER FOUR

10 Common Job Interview Mistakes and How to Avoid Them

From all we have been exploring, you have started noting some things to avoid during the process of a job interview. There are some mistakes that constantly reoccur, especially among fresh graduates who are having their first interview. Let's go through them now, along with how to avoid them, so you can land yourself that job.

The ten most common job interview mistakes are as follows:

- Overconfidence

  It is common for job interview candidates to become too confident after they have read a lot of resources on how to be confident at a job interview. It is not impressive to have low confidence, but it is equally a turnoff if you are too confident. You don't want to leave your interviewer feeling intimidated by you. Be confident enough to express yourself boldly, but make sure you strike a balance because there is just a thin line between being very confident and being arrogant.

- **Performing Instead of Being Natural**

  It is true that you are encouraged to rehearse for your interview. You are even advised to have a mock interview before the main one. But the goal is not to recite a script, but instead to have the interview flow naturally. The aim of the pre- interview practice is for you to get used to what you are supposed to do. Don't memorize lines, internalize them. You may be wondering how your interviewer can tell the difference. It is always easy to tell when someone is faking it. For one, the particular scripts you will memorize may not exactly answer the question you are asked, and you may end up answering in line with your script but not in line with the question you are asked. Use the suggestions in this book to learn how to respond to interview questions, but be prepared to make your own answers as original as possible.

- **Sharing Too Much Information**

  This usually happens during the question, "Tell me about yourself." Some interviewees get really carried away and start giving details about their personal life, details that may not go down well with the recruiter. Be direct when answering the questions, you are asked and make sure the details you give buttress this direct answer.

- **Having Negative Body Language**

  Body language is usually a result of the posture you have over time. If you know you generally do not give off positive body language, you should put in a lot of time practicing how to sit and talk face-to-face with someone. Get someone else to monitor your body language as you do.

- **Trash-Talking Your Former Employer**

  If you have had a job experience which was not palatable, you should not bring it up unless you need to explain a gap in your work life or the reason you spent a short time at a certain workplace. Whichever is the case, please do not say anything negative about your former employer. However you portray your former employer will give the recruiter insight into how you will talk about them should your relationship with them go wrong as well. No matter what may have happened, if you must talk about it, do not do it from a perspective of criticism.

- **Getting Too Excited**

  During your research, you may find out a lot of interesting things about the company that may get you really excited. For instance, if you learn that the company has a good work culture and the staff is happy, you may become so excited about the company that you won't say much about the position. There is also another case of losing perspective because you have been called for a role slightly different from what you applied for. For instance, if you applied for the position of a digital marketer and you are called in for a content marketing interview, content marketing is an offshoot of digital marketing, and as you are answering questions, you should be able to convince the recruiter that you know the relationship between them. Shouldn't you talk about the position you were called in for vs. the position you applied for? Meaning if you were called in for content marketing, you should talk about that, and not get carried away with talking about digital marketing, even though that was the job you originally wanted.

- **Asking Unintelligent Questions or No Questions At All**

  Once you are given the opportunity to ask questions, please don't say you do not have any questions. You should have prepared a few questions from your research before coming to the interview. And even during the course of the interview, you should have noticed one or two points that you need clarifications on. So ask your questions. But please ensure that your first question is not about money to avoid coming across to the recruiter as a money-oriented person.

- **Flirting with the Recruiter**

I assume you know better than to flirt with your recruiter, so let's take this as a reminder. Do not for any reason flirt with your interviewer, especially if they are of the opposite sex. Avoid commenting on their cologne or anything they have on their body. Concentrate on what the business of the day is. The only compliment you owe your interviewer is a hello and a smile.

- **Telling Lies**

  This is an absolute no-no. You should be very honest throughout your interview process. You may package yourself very well for the role, but make sure there are no lies lurking anywhere around that packaging. It is very possible for you to get a job by lying about your qualifications and skills, but those lies will eventually catch up with you, and you may lose the job. Which is more painful, to not get the job, or to lose it as a result of the lies you have told? Your guess is as good as mine.

- **Not Asking What the Next Step Is**

  It is expected that at the end of your interview session, you will ask for the contact information of your interviewer as well as confirm with them what the next step is. This will give them the impression that you always plan ahead, and may improve your chances of being called back.

CONCLUSION

In as much as there is no one-size-fits-all method to acing a job interview, clearly because jobs and interviewers differ, there is a regular pattern that informed all the suggestions in this book. If you closely follow the advice I have given, it will work for you like it has worked for others.

Prepare for your interview ahead of time. Practice responses to the questions in this book, but remember you should not memorize them. They are here to guide you. I intentionally provided very few live instances to make sure you don't memorize them. You need to learn how to respond, build your confidence, and attend any interview fearlessly and boldly. By the time you get your dream job, you may even be ready to start teaching other job seekers how to do well at a job interview.

This book, however, will not be beneficial for you if you just tuck it away without following the guidelines. As the saying goes, you will remain exactly where you are today, even five years from now, except for the books you read and the people you meet. But I want to add that you can read books and still remain how you are unless you practice what you learn from those books. I wish you the best with your job hunting!

First of all, thank you for purchasing this book GET THAT JOB! ACE Your JOB Interview – Every Time! I know you could have picked any number of books to read, but you chose this book and for that I am extremely grateful.

If you enjoyed this book and found some benefit in reading this, I'd like to hear from you and hope that you could take some time to post a review on Amazon. Your feedback and support will be appreciated.

You can follow this link Quick Review on Amazon now.

It only takes a minute and it would mean a lot!

For more Tips to Starting College visit:

Tips to Starting College

Job Application

WORKBOOK

Current Job Applications

JOB TITLE	COMPANY	DEADLINE	DATE APPLIED	RESPONSE	DETAILS

Application Deadlines

JOB TITLE	COMPANY	SOURCE	APPLICATIONS OPEN	DEADLINE	APPLIED

Application Profile

COMPANY NAME: DATE APPLIED:

POSITION TITLE: OVERALL OUTCOME:

Progress Tracker

INITIAL APPLICATION AND METHOD:	Date:

THEIR STEP, MY ACTION AND OUTCOME:	Date:

THEIR STEP, MY ACTION AND OUTCOME:	Date:

THEIR STEP, MY ACTION AND OUTCOME:	Date:

THEIR STEP, MY ACTION AND OUTCOME:	Date

THEIR STEP, MY ACTION AND OUTCOME:	Date:

Company Research

COMPANY NAME :   COMPANY SIZE :

COMPANY SECTOR/INDUSTRY :   INTERVIEW DATE :

WHAT DOES THE COMPANY DO?

HAS THE COMPANY BEEN IN THE NEWS RECENTLY? HAVE THEY MADE ANY HEADLINES?

DOES THE COMPANY HAVE A REPUTATION IN ITS INDUSTRY, OR IN GENERAL? IS THIS GOOD OR BAD?

DOES THE COMPANY GET INVOLVED IN ANY CHARITY/NONPROFIT ACTIVITIES? DO THEY SUPPORT EMPLOYEES WHO DO? DO THEY HAVE ENVIRONMENTAL OR OTHER SIMILAR INITIATIVES?

IS THE EMPLOYEE ATMOSPHERE COLLABORATIVE OR COMPETITIVE? IS IT A TEAM OR INDIVIDUAL BASED ENVIRONMENT?

WHAT COMPANY CULTURE AND VALUES DO THEY PROMOTE? WHAT DO THEY MARKET THEMSELVES ON?

IS THERE SCOPE FOR PROGRESSION/PROMOTION? CAN EMPLOYEES MOVE AROUND THE COMPANY?

Company And Role Questions

COMPANY NAME :   POSITION TITLE :

WHY DO YOU WANT TO WORK FOR THIS COMPANY?

HOW DO THIS COMPANY AND POSITION FIT INTO YOUR CAREER AMBITIONS?

WHY WILL YOU FIT IN AT THIS COMPANY?

WHY DO YOU WANT TO WORK IN THIS INDUSTRY? WHAT DREW YOU TO THIS INDUSTRY?

WHAT DO YOU THINK YOUR DAY-TO-DAY ROLE MIGHT ENTAIL?

WHAT MAKES YOU PERFECT FOR THIS ROLE?

Additional Research

Need more space to elaborate on research, e.g. on a company, or found some more questions you want to ask (and answer)? You can do that here

Company And Role Questions

COMPANY NAME :   POSITION TITLE :

WHY DO YOU WANT TO WORK FOR THIS COMPANY?

HOW DO THIS COMPANY AND POSITION FIT INTO YOUR CAREER AMBITIONS?

WHY WILL YOU FIT IN AT THIS COMPANY?

WHY DO YOU WANT TO WORK IN THIS INDUSTRY? WHAT DREW YOU TO THIS INDUSTRY?

WHAT DO YOU THINK YOUR DAY-TO-DAY ROLE MIGHT ENTAIL?

WHAT MAKES YOU PERFECT FOR THIS ROLE?

Traditional Interview Questions

NAME :   TITLE :

WHAT DO YOU CONSIDER TO BE YOUR BIGGEST STRENGTH?

WHAT DO YOU CONSIDER TO BE YOUR BIGGEST WEAKNESS?

WHERE DO YOU SEE YOURSELF IN FIVE YEARS?

WHAT KIND OF WORK ENVIRONMENT SUITS YOU BEST? DO YOU PREFER COMPETITION OR COLLABORATION?

WHY DO YOU WANT TO LEAVE YOUR CURRENT ROLE?

DO YOU CONSIDER YOURSELF TO BE A GOOD LEADER?

Core Competency Questions

NAME :   POSITION TITLE :

GIVE AN EXAMPLE OF A TIME YOU AND A CO-WORKER DISAGREED ON HOW TO MOVE FORWARD

TELL US ABOUT A TIME YOU'VE HAD TO COMMUNICATE A MESSAGE TO A NUMBER OF DIFFERENT STAKEHOLDERS

DESCRIBE A TIME YOU RESOLVED A CONFLICT BETWEEN CO-WORKERS

GIVE AN EXAMPLE OF A TIME YOU PROVIDED EXEMPLARY CUSTOMER SERVICE

DESCRIBE A TIME YOU HAD TO MANAGE A LARGE WORKLOAD OR NUMEROUS PROJECTS SIMULTANEOUSLY

GIVE AN EXAMPLE OF A TIME YOU TOOK THE INITIATIVE AND WENT BEYOND YOUR JOB DESCRIPTION

Additional Questions

FOUND MORE APPLICATION FORM/INTERVIEW QUESTIONS YOU WANT TO PREPARE FOR?
DRAFT SOME ANSWERS HERE:

Questions to Ask at an Interview

COMPANY NAME: _____ INTERVIEW DATE: _____

POSITION TITLE: _____ JOB TITLE: _____

<u>SOME EXAMPLES:</u>

Can you tell me more about the team I'll be working with?

What drew you to this company? How did you get started with this company?

What do you enjoy about working at this company?

Is there scope for progression in this role/at this company?

Can you tell me more about the day-to-day work I'd be doing in this role?

is there scope for further training & development as part of this role/in this company?

What is the next step in the application process?

MIND-MAP SOME MORE IDEAS HERE:

Useful Websites

WEBSITES	TYPE OF SITES	USER NAME/EMAIL	PASSWORD

Notes

Made in the USA
Coppell, TX
17 January 2021